A Guide for Using

The Tale of Despereaux

in the Classroom

Based on the novel written by Kate DiCamillo

This guide written by
Melissa Hart, M.F.A.

Teacher Created Resources, Inc.
6421 Industry Way
Westminster, CA 92683
www.teachercreated.com
ISBN: 978-1-4206-3164-7
©2005 Teacher Created Resources, Inc.
Reprinted, 2009
Made in U.S.A.

Edited by
Sara Connolly

Illustrated by
Sue Fullam

Cover Art by
Kevin Barnes

Table of Contents

Introduction

A good book can enrich our lives like a good friend. Fictional characters can inspire us and teach us about the world in which we live. We may turn to books for companionship, entertainment, and guidance. A truly beloved book may touch our lives forever.

Great care has been taken with Literature Units to select books that are sure to become your students' good friends!

Teachers who use this unit will find the following features to supplement their own ideas:

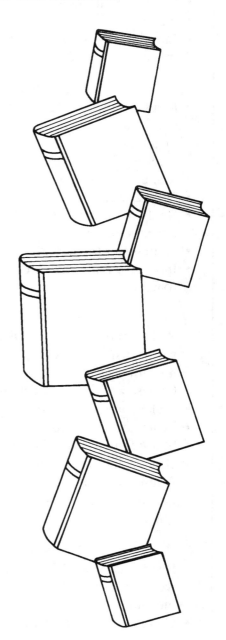

- Sample Lesson Plans

- Pre-Reading Activities

- A Biographical Sketch and Picture of the Author

- A Book Summary

- Vocabulary Lists and Suggested Vocabulary Activities

- Chapters grouped for study with each section including

  — *quizzes*

  — *hands-on projects*

  — *cooperative learning activities*

  — *cross-curricular connections*

  — *extensions into the reader's life*

- Post-Reading Activities

- Book Report Ideas

- Research Activities

- Culminating Activities

- Three Different Options for Unit Tests

- Bibliography

- Answer Key

We are certain this unit will be a valuable addition to your own curriculum ideas to supplement *The Tale of Despereaux*.

Sample Lesson Plans

The time it takes to complete the suggested lessons below will vary, depending on the type of activity, your students' abilities, and their interest levels.

Lesson 1
- Introduce and complete some or all of the pre-reading activities from "Before the Book." (page 5)
- Read "About the Author" with students. (page 6)
- Introduce the vocabulary list for Section 1. (page 8)

Lesson 2
- Read Chapters 1–12. Discuss vocabulary words, using the book's context to discern meanings.
- Choose a vocabulary activity. (page 9)
- Make a handkerchief. (page 11)
- Hold a trial. (page 12)
- Study the Code of Chivalry. (page 13)
- Discuss non-conformists. (page 14)
- Administer the Section 1 Quiz. (page 10)
- Introduce the vocabulary list for Section 2. (page 8)

Lesson 3
- Read Chapters 13–22. Discuss vocabulary words, using the book's context to discern meanings.
- Choose a vocabulary activity. (page 9)
- Make soup. (page 16)
- Learn to juggle. (page 17)
- Study famous dungeons. (page 18)
- Discuss light and darkness. (page 19)
- Administer the Section 2 Quiz. (page 15)
- Introduce the vocabulary list for Section 3. (page 8)

Lesson 4
- Read Chapters 23-33. Discuss vocabulary words, using the book's context to discern meanings.
- Choose a vocabulary activity. (page 9)
- Weave a tapestry. (page 21)
- Notice sensory details. (page 22)
- Research kings, soldiers, and servants. (page 23)

- Discuss hope and planning. (page 24)
- Administer the Section 3 Quiz. (page 20)
- Introduce the vocabulary list for Section 4. (page 8)

Lesson 5
- Read Chapters 34–43. Discuss vocabulary words, using the book's context to discern meanings.
- Choose a vocabulary activity. (page 9)
- Make your own storybook. (page 26)
- Research famous quests. (page 27)
- Create a maze. (page 28)
- Learn about empathy. (page 29)
- Administer the Section 4 Quiz. (page 25)
- Introduce the vocabulary list for Section 5. (page 8)

Lesson 6
- Read Chapters 44–Coda. Discuss vocabulary words, using the book's context to discern meanings.
- Choose a vocabulary activity. (page 9)
- Make a diorama. (page 31)
- Learn to trust your senses. (page 32)
- Research foreign words. (page 33)
- Examine consequences. (page 34)
- Administer the Section 4 Quiz. (page 30)

Lesson 7
- Discuss questions students have about the book. (page 35)
- Assign a book report and research activity. (pages 36–37)
- Begin work on one or more culminating activities. (pages 38–42)

Lesson 8
- Choose and administer one or more of the Unit Tests. (page 43–45)
- Discuss students' feelings about the book.
- Provide a bibliography of related reading. (page 46)

Before the Book

Before you begin reading *The Tale of Despereaux* with your students, complete one or more of the following pre-reading activities to stimulate their interest and enhance comprehension.

1. Examine the cover of the book. Ask students to predict the book's plot, character, and setting.

2. Discuss the title. Does the root, "desper" bring to mind words such as "despair," "desperate," and "disappointment"? See if students can predict anything from the title.

3. Pose the following questions and ask students to respond:

    *   Have you ever felt like a disappointment to your parents?

    *   Have you ever acted in a manner different from that of your brothers and sisters?

    *   What would it feel like to be sent to prison?

    *   How might it feel to be treated poorly because of the way you look?

    *   What would you do in order to save someone you love?

    *   Have you ever wished to be something you just couldn't be?

    *   How would you feel if you lost someone dear to you?

    *   What might it feel like to not have a mother?

    *   Can you think of a time in which you forgave someone who had hurt you, and do you remember how it felt to forgive that person?

4. Direct students to work in groups to brainstorm how people are treated because of their appearance and how prejudice might be handled.

5. Ask students to work in groups to list the different reasons that someone might want to cause someone else suffering. Discuss how the person might best be helped in order to change his/her behavior.

6. Direct students to work in groups to brainstorm how you might best save someone who has been kidnapped. Would you go to the police? Post signs with the missing person's picture? Would you try to find the person yourself?

7. Have students work in groups to make a list of what they know about fairy tales — specifically those pertaining to castles, knights, and courtly love. Compare the lists and share the findings with the class.

About the Author

Kate DiCamillo was born in Philadelphia, Pennsylvania. She had a difficult childhood. When she was five years old, her father left her family. She also suffered from chronic pneumonia. A doctor advised her mother to move Kate to a warmer climate, where her health would improve. That year, Kate found herself living in Florida!

As a child, Kate always wanted to write and tell stories. Some of her favorite childhood books were *The Yearling*, *Ribsy*, and *The Secret Garden*. After graduating from the University of Florida with a degree in English, she went to work for Disney World. She also called bingo at a children's camp. In her twenties, she told people she was a writer; however, she hadn't yet written anything. Then, she moved from Florida to Minnesota, where she took a job at a children's bookstore.

That first cold winter was hard on Kate; she was far away from home, and it was the first time she didn't own a dog. However, she turned what could have been a very dark time into something positive. Waking up at four a.m. every morning, she wrote a book for children, titled *Because of Winn-Dixie*. This book, about a girl who adopts a stray dog, won a Newbery Honor. Kate says that after she found out that she won the award, she spent the whole day "walking into walls."

Kate followed *Because of Winn-Dixie* with another novel, *The Tiger Rising*, about a boy who discovers a tiger living in the woods behind the Kentucky Star Hotel. *The Tale of Despereaux* is Kate's third novel. Her best friend's son asked her to write a book about a hero with "exceptionally large" ears, so she wrote about a mouse, Despereaux, who is in love with a princess. The novel won the Newbery Award for children's literature.

Kate is currently at work on several books for young people. She writes at least two pages every morning, five days a week. She has worked with a critique group of writers for five years. They read each other's writing aloud every other week and comment on it. She receives a great deal of fan mail from her readers and tries to respond to every letter.

You can find out more about Kate DiCamillo on her publisher's website at **www.candlewick.com**. There, she notes this about her passion for writing: "E. B. White said, 'All that I hope to say in books, all that I ever hope to say, is that I love the world.'" Kate adds, "That's the way I feel too."

The Tale of Despereaux

By Kate DiCamillo
(Candlewick Press, 2003)

This book is written in four parts. Book One, "A Mouse is Born," tells the story of the birth of Despereaux, the only baby in his mother's litter to survive. He disappoints his family members when he shows no interest in learning to scurry or search for crumbs. He knows how to read, and he loves music so much that he allows King Phillip and Princess Pea to see him. Despereaux falls in love with the princess, but his father sees him talking to humans and calls a meeting of the Mouse Council, who sentence him to death in the dungeon. In the dungeon, Despereaux meets the jailer, Gregory, who asks the mouse to tell him a story and thus, saves his life.

Book Two, "Chiaroscuro," introduces the rat, Roscuro, who loves light so much that he creeps upstairs and climbs into a chandelier. When Princess Pea surprises him, Roscuro falls into a bowl of soup and Queen Rosemary dies. Roscuro hears himself called a rat, and his heart breaks. He resolves to make others suffer as much as he is suffering.

In Book Three, "Gor! The Tale of Miggery Sow," Miggery Sow is a poor, motherless girl sold into slavery. The king's soldier discovers her and takes her to the castle, where she becomes a servant. She meets Princess Pea and decides that she wants to become a princess, as well. In the dungeon, Roscuro befriends Miggery and tells her of a plan in which she can take Pea's place as princess.

Book Four, "Recalled to the Light," follows Roscuro as he persuades Miggery Sow to help him kidnap the princess and take her to the dungeon. Meanwhile, Despereaux realizes it is up to him to save Princess Pea. The cook offers him a bowl of illegal soup. While searching for a spool of red thread, Despereaux comes upon his father, whom he forgives for sending him to the dungeon. Then the mouse, guided by the rat, Botticelli Remorso, winds his way into the dungeon in search of Princess Pea.

After near-tragedy, all is forgiven. Despereaux earns a place of honor beside Princess Pea, Roscuro earns a bowl of soup, and even Miggery Sow ends up nearly a princess.

Vocabulary Lists

Below are lists of vocabulary words for each section of chapters. A variety of ideas for using this vocabulary in classroom activities is offered on page 9.

Section 1 (Chapters 1–12)

diplomat	consorts
speculation	fervent
indignant	renounce
fate	perfidy
conform	egregious
captivating	decree
tribunal	repent
staccato	ominous
indisputable	hood

Section 2 (Chapters 13–22)

abyss	tiresome
implications	despicable
all-encompassing	astute
callused	solace
beleaguered	minstrels
irony	consigned
treacherous	ornate
prophecy	palate
inordinate	revenge

Section 3 (Chapters 23–33)

dire	dour	portentous
consequence	tapestry	ascertaining
outlaw	permeated	aspirations
torturous	bungle	
clout	olfactory	
scrupulous	discernable	
innumerable	pronouncement	

Section 4 (Chapters 34–43)

philosophy	pance	diminishment
recalled	understatement	meditative
gratitude	defiant	quest
covert	ignorant	lair
institute	empathy	beatific
divine	rubbish	
comeup-	earnest	

Section 5 (Chapters 44–Coda)

inspiring	rumors	access
emboldened	thwarted	atone
extraordinary	vengeful	
maneuvering	infringe	
gnarled	consigned	
cornucopia	heartily	
exaggerated	anticipated	

8

Vocabulary Activity Ideas

You can help your students learn the vocabulary words in *The Tale of Despereaux* by providing them with the stimulating vocabulary activities below.

1. Ask your students to work in groups to create an **Illustrated Book** of the vocabulary words and their meanings.

2. Separate students into groups. Use the vocabulary words to create **Crossword Puzzles** and **Word Searches**. Groups can trade puzzles with each other, and solve them.

3. Play **Guess the Definition**. One student writes down the correct definition of the vocabulary word. The others write down false definitions, close enough to the original definition that their classmates might be fooled. Read all definitions, and then challenge students to guess the correct one. The students whose definitions mislead their classmates get a point for each student fooled. Use the word in five different sentences. Compare sentences and discuss.

4. Write a **Short Story** using as many of the words as possible. Students may then read their stories in groups.

5. Encourage your students to use each new vocabulary word in a Conversation five times during one day. They can take notes on how and when the word was used, and then share their experience with the class.

6. Play **Vocabulary Charades**. Each student or group of students gets a word to act out. Other students must guess the word.

7. Play **Vocabulary Pictures**. Each student or group of students must draw a picture representing a word on the chalkboard or on paper. Other students must guess the word.

8. Challenge students to a **Vocabulary Bee**. In groups or separately, students must spell the word correctly, and give its proper definition.

9. Talk about **Parts of Speech** by discussing the different forms that a word may take. For instance, some words may function as nouns, as well as verbs. The word "honor" is a good example of a word which can be both a noun and a verb. Some words which look alike may have completely different meanings; in *The Tale of Despereaux*, the word "hood" refers to the hooded mice who escort Despereaux to the dungeon, but it may also refer to a criminal.

10. Ask your students to make **Flash Cards** with the word printed on one side and the definition printed on the other. Students may work with a younger class to help them learn the definitions of the new words, using the flash cards.

11. Create **Word Art** by writing the words with glue on stiff paper, and then cover the glue with glitter or sand. Alternatively, students may write the words with a squeeze bottle full of jam on bread to create an edible lesson!

Quiz Time

Answer the following questions about chapters 1 through 11.

1. Why is Antoinette disappointed in her son? _____

    _____

    _____

2. How is Despereaux different from other mice? _____

    _____

    _____

3. What do Despereaux's siblings try to teach him? _____

    _____

    _____

4. Why can't Despereaux nibble on the book? _____

    _____

    _____

5. Why does Despereaux reveal himself to the King and the Princess?

    _____

    _____

6. What happens when Pea smiles at Despereaux? _____

    _____

    _____

7. Why do the other mice say Despereaux cannot be trusted? _____

    _____

    _____

8. Why doesn't Lester defend his son? _____

    _____

    _____

Make a Handkerchief

Several of the characters in *The Tale of Despereaux* use handkerchiefs—pieces of cloth on which to blow their noses and wipe their eyes. You can sew your own handkerchief and personalize it with simple embroidery.

Materials

- one square of pre-washed cotton, 10" x 10", for each student
- one needle and a spool of thread for each student
- scissors
- scratch paper
- pencils
- embroidery needles and floss

(**Note to teacher:** a blunt #22 safety needle is recommended)

Directions

1. Give each student a square of cotton. Students should hem all sides of the square by folding over one inch on each side and sewing the hem in place. (See illustration.)

2. When handkerchiefs are hemmed, ask students to design a decoration on scratch paper with a pencil. The decoration might be a symbol, their initials, or a border of some sort that distinguishes each student's handkerchief from the others.

3. Lightly trace the decoration on the cotton with a pencil, hem-side down. Then, thread the embroidery needle with floss and embroider the decoration, using the cross-stitch described below.

4. The beginning half of a full cross-stitch creates a half stitch. Working from right to left, bring the needle up from the back at position 1, down at 2, up at 3, down at 4, and so on.

5. Begin as above (half-stitch), working from right to left (as shown). Complete the stitch by returning from left to right. Bring the needle up from the back at position 5, down at 6, up at 7, down at 8, etc. Be sure the needle goes up and down in a corner hole cleanly, so that none of the threads from previous stitches are split apart.

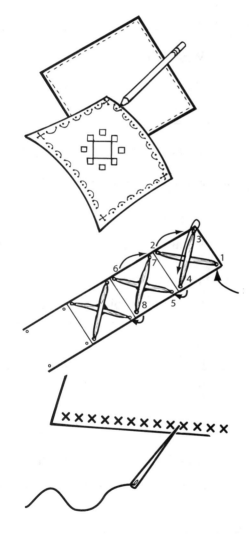

Tip: You may stitch left to right, right to left, or top to bottom, as long as all your bottom half stitches lay in one direction and the finishing top cross stitches lay in the opposite direction.

Hold a Trial

Despereaux is brought to trial in a tribunal held by the Mouse Council. The council is made up of thirteen honored mice and one Most Very Honored Head Mouse, who accuse Despereaux of serious crimes before banishing him to the dungeon.

Use encyclopedias, books, and Internet search engines to research contemporary trial procedures. Answer the following questions:

1. How many jurors hear a trial? How are they chosen?

   _____

   _____

2. What is the role of lawyers in a trial? Should Despereaux have had a lawyer?

   _____

   _____

3. What is the role of the judge? How does the jury's verdict affect the judge's decision?

   _____

   _____

4. What is the role of court reporter?

   _____

5. What is the role of the bailiff?

   _____

6. How are witnesses brought to trial, and what are they obligated to reveal, and to whom?

   _____

   _____

7. Can the public observe a trial?

   _____

Now that you've learned more about judicial process, hold a mock trial in your classroom. Assign students to play the part of prosecutors, defendants, witnesses, jurors, bailiff, court reporter, lawyers, and judge. Don't forget to assign someone the role of "threadmaster." Take some time to develop a script for Despereaux's trial, based on what you've read in the novel.

Finally, act out the trial. You may want to videotape it for later viewing, or invite students from another class to watch you. Consider acting out Despereaux's trial for an Open House night at your school.

The Code of Chivalry

Despereaux reads a fairy tale about knights and maidens. When the threadmaster finds out that the little mouse is in love with Princess Pea, he says, "And you love her, as a knight loves a maiden. You love her with a courtly love, with a love that is based on bravery and courtesy and honor and devotion."

Chivalry was a code of honor followed by medieval knights, most frequently in the 12th and 13th centuries. Using encyclopedias, books, and/or the Internet, answer the following questions about the code of chivalry.

1. How did a boy become a knight in medieval times?

   _____

   _____

2. How was a squire welcomed into the order of knights?

   _____

   _____

3. What did a knight wear on his chest during battle? Why?

   _____

   _____

4. What types of things did a knight do to win the affections of a lady in the feudal court?

   _____

   _____

5. Why did knights fight tournaments at court?

   _____

   _____

6. What did the Code of Chivalry say about the following:

   a. Loyalty _____

   b. Defense _____

   c. Courage _____

   d. Faith _____

   e. Courtesy _____

Being a Non-Conformist

Despereaux is a non-conformist—that is, he behaves differently from the other mice. He refuses to nibble the pages of books, isn't interested in searching for crumbs, and he shocks his family by allowing himself to be seen by humans. When he is caught talking to a human, the Mouse Council sentences him to the dungeon.

Think about a time that you were a non-conformist. What led you to behave differently from everyone else? How did other people react? How did you feel? What did you learn from your experience?

Write two paragraphs, below, describing your experience as a non-conformist.

Quiz Time

Answer the following questions about chapters 13 through 22.

1. How does Despereaux's mother react to her son being sentenced to the dungeon?

_____

_____

2. What does Despereaux discover about one of the hoods who escorts him to the dungeon?

_____

_____

3. Who is Gregory?

_____

_____

4. What does Gregory ask Despereaux to do?

_____

_____

5. Why does Roscuro go upstairs to the party?

_____

_____

6. Why does Queen Rosemary die?

_____

_____

7. Why doesn't Roscuro like being called a rat?

_____

_____

8. What happens to Roscuro when he looks over his shoulder at Princess Pea?

_____

_____

A Masterwork of Soup

Note to Teacher: Send home a written note with students, inquiring about pertinent food allergies, well in advance of preparing this soup.

Queen Rosemary loves soup, and the last bowl she ever enjoys is a masterwork of chicken, watercress, and garlic. You, too, can create this soup, with just a few simple ingredients.

This recipe makes enough soup for 30 people.

Ingredients

- 5 tablespoons vegetable oil
- 5 potatoes, peeled and cubed
- 5 small onions, chopped
- 5 cloves of garlic, minced or pressed
- 1 ¼ teaspoon salt
- 1 ¼ teaspoon ground black pepper
- 12 ½ cups chicken stock
- 12 ½ cups milk or plain soy milk
- 7 ½ pounds watercress, large stems removed

Materials

- large soup pot
- cutting board
- knife
- wooden spoon
- vegetable peeler
- blender or food processor
- individual soup bowls and spoons

Directions

1. Heat oil in soup pot over medium-high heat. Stir in chopped potato, onions, and garlic. Season with salt and pepper. Reduce heat to medium, cover, and simmer for five minutes.

2. Pour in chicken stock and milk, bringing mixture to a gentle boil. Reduce heat to low and simmer for 10 minutes, until potatoes are tender. Stir in watercress.

3. Transfer soup in small batches to a blender and puree until smooth. (Hold a towel firmly over the top of the blender to prevent splashes.)

4. Pour soup into individual bowls and garnish with springs of watercress. Enjoy!

Let's Juggle!

Roscuro creeps into the banquet hall of the palace and discovers a wonderful party.

> "Everything glittered. Everything. The gold spoons on the table and the jingle bells on the juggler's cap, the strings on the minstrels' guitars and the crowns on the king's and queen's heads."
>   —*The Tale of Despereaux*

Juggling has been a popular form of entertainment for centuries. Jesters entertained kings and queens with their juggling skills. With just a little practice and the help of a partner, you'll become a skillful juggler, too!

Materials

Three balls, about the size and weight of a small apple

Directions

1. Choose a partner, and decide which of you will go first. Now, imagine two focus spots, one to the right, and one to the left, about a foot in front of your forehead. Hold your arms at waist level with your hands out naturally in front of you. Start with a ball in your right hand, and your left hand empty. Toss the ball across to the focus spot on your left and catch the ball in your left hand. Your partner should call out "left." Now, toss it gently to the focus spot on your right and catch it in your right hand. Your partner should call out "right."

2. Then hold two balls in your right hand—one at the base of your fingers, and one at the back of your palm. Hold the third ball in your left hand. Toss the first ball from the base of your fingers toward your left hand. Your partner calls out "left." When the ball starts on its way down, toss the second ball from your left hand and catch the first ball in your left hand as it comes down. Your partner calls out "left" again. Catch the second ball in your right hand, with your partner calling out "right." Practice until you can do this easily, remembering to concentrate on your focus spots. You're almost juggling!

3. Now, repeat the second step, above. But this time, as the second ball is on its way down, toss the third ball from your right hand and catch it in your left. Toss the balls from the inside of your hands, and catch them on the outside. To keep your timing consistent, your partner should call out "left" and "right" as you throw from each hand. Practice until you can consistently catch the balls.

4. Repeat the step above, adding one more toss each time you get comfortable with a series of exchanges. Then, allow your partner to take a turn. When both of you are proficient at basic juggling, you can practice juggling balls higher, lower, standing on one foot, and tossing them to each other in a rhythmic pattern!

Famous Dungeons

Despereaux is thrown into a dungeon, where he meets Gregory, the dungeon-master. Roscuro also lives in the dungeon with all the other rats. In order to get a better idea of where these characters live, research famous dungeons from across the ages.

Get into groups of three. Using encyclopedias, books, and/or the Internet, answer the following questions about these famous dungeons. Then, share your answers with your class.

The Tower of London

1. Where was it located? _____

2. In what year was it built? _____

3. Who built it? _____

4. Who was held prisoner here? _____

5. List three interesting facts about this dungeon. _____

Kaiserburg Castle

1. Where was it located? _____

2. In what year was it built? _____

3. Who built it? _____

4. Who was held prisoner here? _____

5. List three interesting facts about this dungeon. _____

The Bastille

1. Where was it located? _____

2. In what year was it built? _____

3. Who built it? _____

4. Who was held prisoner here? _____

5. List three interesting facts about this dungeon. _____

Mamertine Prison

1. Where was it located? _____

2. In what year was it built? _____

3. Who was held prisoner here? _____

4. List three interesting facts about this dungeon. _____

   Extra Credit: Who built it? _____

Light and Darkness

In the dungeon, Roscuro gets his first glimpse of light. "I think," said Roscuro, "that the meaning of life is light."

"Light," said Botticelli. "Ha-ha-ha—you kill me. Light has nothing to do with it."

Review chapters 16–20 and think further about what life means to Roscuro, as compared to Botticelli. Then answer the questions below in detailed, complete paragraphs.

1. What is the meaning of life for Roscuro before he lands in the Queen's soup?

_____

_____

_____

_____

2. What is the meaning of life for Botticelli?

_____

_____

_____

_____

3. What is the meaning of life for Despereaux?

_____

_____

_____

_____

4. What is the meaning of life for you?

_____

_____

_____

_____

Quiz Time

Answer the following questions about chapters 23 through 33.

1. What happens to Miggery Sow's ears?

   _____

   _____

2. Who is Miggery's father, and where does he live now?

   _____

   _____

3. How does Miggery feel after she sees the royal family?

   _____

   _____

4. Why is Miggery sent to the castle to work?

   _____

   _____

5. How are Miggery and Princess Pea similar?

   _____

   _____

6. How are Miggery and Princess Pea different?

   _____

   _____

7. Why doesn't the dungeon bother Miggery?

   _____

   _____

8. Who do you think is hiding in the napkin on Gregory's tray?

   _____

   _____

Make a Tapestry

Miggery Sow sees that Princess Pea is making a tapestry that shows the history of her world. Pea's father, the king, is playing guitar. Her mother is eating soup.

The art of tapestry has been around hundreds of years. Often, it involves weaving. Some weavers use straw, some use gold, and others, like Princess Pea, use thread. You can make a simple woven tapestry using strips of colored paper which you can then decorate with pictures that show the history of your world. When you are finished with your tapestry, sign your name in the lower right corner and display it on a bulletin board for others to enjoy!

Materials

- at least two 8" x 11" pieces of colored paper for each student

- pencil

- ruler

- scissors

- transparent tape or glue

- one piece of black paper, 8" x 11", for each student

- markers or crayons

Directions

1. First, draw seven horizontal lines, each an inch apart on a piece of colored paper. Then, carefully cut along those lines, leaving an inch at both ends of each of the lines uncut. (See diagram.)

2. Now, cut 11 strips of colored paper. Each strip should be 1" x 8". You may choose to use all one color, or mix colors.

3. When you have 11 strips, begin to weave one into your large piece of paper. (See diagram.) Weave all 11 strips, side by side.

4. After you have woven your tapestry, cut a piece of black paper into strips—two 1" x 11" strips and two 1" x 8" strips. Tape or glue these strips around the edges of your tapestry to make a frame.

5. Finally, use markers or crayons to draw your history on your tapestry. What symbols can you draw to show the people, animals, places, and other objects that are important to you?

Sensory Details

The Tale of Despereaux is rich with sensory details—that is, details that appeal to the reader's five senses: touch, taste, smell, sight, and hearing. Consider this description of the dungeon:

"It was quiet in an ominous way; it was quiet in the way of small, frightening sounds. There was the snail-like slither of water oozing down the walls and from around the darkened corner there came the low moan of someone groaning in pain. And then, too, there was the noise of the rats going about their business, their sharp nails hitting the stones of the dungeon and their long tails dragging behind them, through the blood and muck."—*The Tale of Despereaux*

Get into groups of three. Read through Section 3 of this novel, and list sensory details on the chart below. A few have been included for you.

touch	sharp nails hitting stones of dungeon			
taste				
smell				
sight	tails dragging through blood and muck			
hearing	groaning in pain	slither of water		

Kings and Soldiers and Servants

In medieval days, countries such as England and Spain were ruled by kings, who commanded regiments of soldiers and were taken care of by servants. Using encyclopedias, books, and the Internet, compare the various roles of these different people, and then explore whether those same roles exist today.

Person	What was this person's job?	How did this person dress?	Is this person rich or poor?	How is this person treated?	Does this type of person still exist today? Explain.
King/Queen					
Prince/ Princess					
Soldier					
Servant					

Hope and Planning

At the end of Chapter 28, the narrator asks,

"Reader, do you think that it is a terrible thing to hope when there is really no reason to hope at all? Or is it (as the soldier said about happiness) something that you might just as well do, since, in the end, it really makes no difference to anyone but you?"

—*The Tale of Despereaux*

Many of the characters in this novel have hope. Despereaux hopes that he will be allowed to serve Princess Pea. Roscuro hopes to take revenge on the Princess. Miggery Sow hopes to become a princess, just like Pea. What do you hope for?

Below, write one paragraph listing three things you hope for. Perhaps you hope for a particular job someday, or a car, or a horse. Maybe you hope for someone in your life to be happy, or you hope to be reunited with someone you've lost.

In your second paragraph, examine how you can make your dreams come true! For instance, if you hope to become an airplane pilot, you can take flying lessons and learn all there is to know about planes. If you hope to travel to Europe to see castles and dungeons and monuments, write about how you plan to get there.

Hope, combined with a plan, is a magical thing. With preparation and dedication, you can make your dreams come true!

Quiz Time

Answer the following questions about chapters 34 through 43.

1. What does Miggery Sow take from Despereaux in the kitchen?

   _____

2. Why does Miggery believe in Roscuro's plan?

   _____

   _____

3. What does Princess Pea dream about her mother?

   _____

4. Why does the princess feel sorry for Miggery?

   _____

   _____

5. What leads to Gregory's death?

   _____

   _____

6. Why does Despereaux forgive his father?

   _____

   _____

7. Why doesn't the king believe Despereaux?

   _____

8. Why does Despereaux want the spool of red thread?

   _____

   _____

   _____

Make Your Own Storybook

Make a Copper Book

In ancient times, people bent and shaped metal in order to make coins, dishes, helmets, and other useful items. You can make a copper cover for a fairy tale that you have written and illustrated.

Materials

- 4 pieces of heavy white paper for each student
- markers and/or pencils
- sheets of copper (available at craft and hardware stores)
- hole punch
- ballpoint pen or wooden stick
- tracing paper
- 1-foot piece of string or ribbon for each student

Directions

1. First, cut a 4" x 7" rectangle out of copper. Then, cut out four 4" x 7" pieces of paper. Fold both the copper rectangle and the pieces of paper in half. With a hole punch, punch two half-moon shaped holes in the fold of your copper rectangle—this is your book cover. Insert the folded paper into the cover and punch half-moon holes into the paper, just as you did with the copper.

2. Now, take the pages out of your cover and lay the copper flat on a hard surface. Using a ballpoint pen or sturdy wooden stick, emboss the copper with pictures to illustrate your book. To emboss titles or names, write them on a piece of tracing paper, then put it face down on the back side of your cover. Trace the words or names hard with your ballpoint pen. Then turn the cover over so that the letters are right-side up.

3. When you are finished embossing your copper cover, write your fairy tale on the folded pieces of paper, and include illustrations. Don't forget a title page with your name!

4. Finally, tie the pages into your copper book cover with a piece of string or ribbon. Display your book for others to read and enjoy.

Famous Quests

Many famous characters in literature and history have undertaken quests, much like that of Despereaux as he attempts to save Princess Pea. A *quest* is a journey full of adventures, taken by a person in search of something or someone.

Get into groups of three. Using encyclopedias, books, and/or the Internet, research these famous quests and the heroes and heroines who have made them. Then, answer the questions below.

1. **Hero: Odysseus**

   What was the goal of his quest? _____

   What challenges did he face on this quest? _____

   Did he accomplish his goal? _____

2. **Heroine: Joan of Arc**

   What was the goal of her quest? _____

   What challenges did she face on this quest? _____

   Did she accomplish her goal? _____

3. **Hero: Sir Galahad**

   What was the goal of his quest? _____

   What challenges did he face on this quest? _____

   Did he accomplish his goal? _____

4. **Heroine: Amelia Earhart**

   What was the goal of her quest? _____

   What challenges did she face on this quest? _____

   Did she accomplish her goal? _____

5. **Hero: Mahatma Gandhi**

   What was the goal of his quest? _____

   What challenges did he face on this quest? _____

   Did he accomplish his goal? _____

6. **Heroine: Harriet Tubman**

   What was the goal of her quest? _____

   What challenges did she face on this quest? _____

   Did she accomplish her goal? _____

Despereaux's Maze

Despereaux asks the threadmaster for the spool of red thread so he will not get lost in the dungeon's dark maze as he searches for Princess Pea.

In the box below, design a maze for Despereaux. Include math equations in different tunnels on your maze. You might include a combination of addition and subtraction problems, and/or division and multiplication problems. Begin by tracing the true path to the princess in pencil, very lightly. Then design tunnels around that path, most of which should dead end. Trace over your completed tunnels with darker pencil or pen. For more help on how to design a maze, type "Mazes for Kids" in to your favorite search engine on the Internet. The first tunnel has been created for you.

When you have finished designing your maze, pass it to a friend to complete. Grade the finished maze for correct answers to the math problems, and congratulate your friend for helping Despereaux to find the princess!

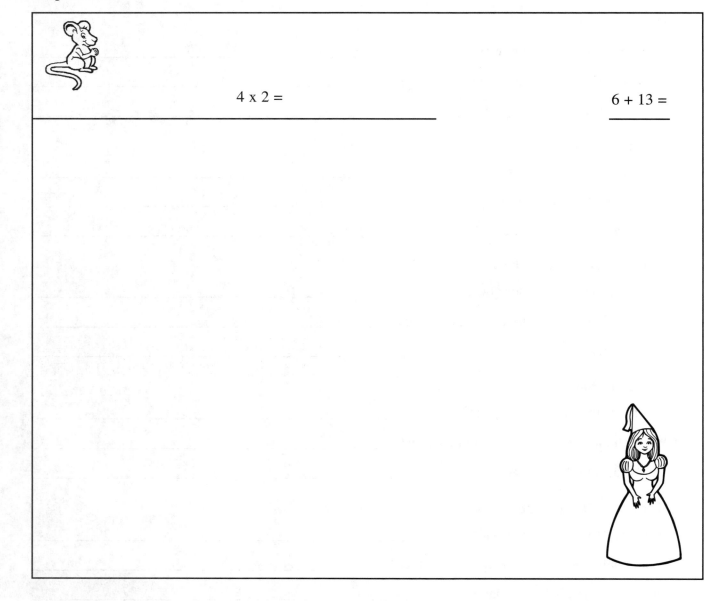

$$4 \times 2 =$$

$$6 + 13 =$$

Being Empathetic

Princess Pea shows empathy—that is, sympathy and compassion—for Miggery Sow when the servant girl leads her down to the dungeon. She proves that a person may be both understanding and forgiving in the midst of anger.

Fill out the following chart to show your understanding of, and empathy for, the difficult characters in *The Tale of Despereaux*. The first one has been completed for you.

Character	Your Understanding of Him/Her
Miggery Sow	*Wants to be a princess so badly that she believes what Roscuro tells her.*
King Phillip	
The Cook	
Roscuro	
Despereaux's father	
Miggery Sow's father	

Now, fill out the following chart to show your understanding of, and empathy for, difficult people in your own life.

Person in Your Life	Your Understanding of Him/Her

Quiz Time

Answer the following questions about chapters 44 through the Coda.

1. Why is the Cook glad to see Despereaux in her kitchen?

_____

_____

_____

2. Why does the Cook's laughter hurt Despereaux?

_____

_____

3. Why does the Cook give Despereaux a bowl of soup?

_____

_____

4. Why does Despereaux follow Boticelli Remorso?

_____

_____

5. What does Despereaux notice about the dungeon?

_____

_____

6. What does the Princess ask Miggery Sow?

_____

7. What does Miggery Sow want?

_____

8. Why does Princess Pea offer Roscuro a bowl of soup?

_____

_____

Make a Diorama

A diorama is a three-dimensional scene set against a decorated background. There are many exciting and descriptive scenes in *The Tale of Despereaux*. Choose your favorite scene from the book and depict it in a diorama.

Materials

- a shoebox with lid
- scissors
- glue
- crayons, paints, pastels,
- sand, dirt, straw, grass, rocks
- molding clay, faux fur, glitter
- colored pencils, and/or markers
- leaves, carpet, and/or felt
- sequins, buttons, and/or fabric

Directions

1. First, sketch the scene you wish to create. What characters will you depict? Think about what lies on the ground in this scene, and what appears in the background Are there interesting objects such as animals or furniture or bones or soup bowls in this scene?

2. Now, remove the lid from your shoebox, and trace characters and objects on the lid. Cut them out and color them appropriately. Make a stand so your characters can stand upright.

3. Place the shoebox on one side. Inside, on the back of the box, draw or paint background scenery. Perhaps you're depicting the final dungeon scene with tufts of fur and mouse bones and bits of red thread, or the scene in which Roscuro falls into the soup during the royal banquet with its gleaming chandelier and jugglers and minstrels

4. Now, glue appropriate ground covering on one side of the box. This may be sand, dirt, straw, grass, etc.

5. Think about how you might create objects out of clay or felt or fabric or other materials.

6. Finally, position your characters inside the box with any objects you feel would be appropriate.

7. Display this diorama of your favorite scene for others to enjoy!

Trust Your Senses

You have noticed how *The Tale of Despereaux* comes alive with sensory descriptions. As Botticelli Remorso leads Despereaux through the dark dungeon, the mouse sees, smells, and feels horrible things. "You must trust me," Botticelli says, and Despereaux does.

The following game is based on trust. Unlike Botticelli, however, your partner will lead you safely and carefully. Your job is to keep all of your senses, except for your eyes and mouth, wide open!

Materials

- blindfold

- short length of rope, about one foot

- paper and pencil

Directions

1. Choose a partner and decide which one of you will be the leader first. The leader should carefully blindfold the follower, making sure he/she can't see.

2. Now, the leader guides the follower for three minutes— holding the length of rope between you— around the classroom or playground. The follower carefully notices sounds, smells, temperature and textures! At the end of three minutes, the follower removes the blindfold and writes down every sensory detail he/she noticed on a piece of paper.

3. Now, switch roles. At the end of three minutes, the new follower writes down sensory details. Compare notes on what you each observed in terms of sound, smell, and touch. Then, share your observations with your class.

   Teacher's Note: For an enhanced experience, set out covered bowls of feathers, clay, gelatin, ice cubes, and other objects to test students' skills in sensory observation.

The Meaning of Words

There are several foreign words, famous European names, and even a fairy tale reference in The Tale of Despereaux. Use a French-English dictionary and/or a free Internet translation program to explain the following words, and an encyclopedia or the Internet to identify the following famous historical or fictional people. The first one has been answered for you.

Botticelli Remorso (famous Italian person)	Botticelli was a famous Italian painter, and the word "remorse" means regret, sorrow, and shame.
Mon Dieu (French phrase)	
merlot (French word)	
furlough (French word)	
C'est moi? (French phrase)	
oui (French word)	
chiaroscuro (Italian word)	
Antoinette (famous French person)	
Princess Pea (famous fairy tale)	
Extra Credit: Identify the root word of the name "Despereaux." Why might Antoinette choose to name her baby this?	

Consequences

The narrator in *The Tale of Despereaux* writes a great deal about consequences. Because Despereaux can read, he learns about courtly love and falls in love with a princess. The consequence of speaking to a human is that he goes to prison, where ultimately, he helps to save Princess Pea's life. Because Roscuro gnaws on Gregory's rope, he learns to love light. The consequence is that he climbs the chandelier, where Princess Pea sees him and cries "Rat," so that he falls into the Queen's soup. Because she dies, the king outlaws soup.

Using the "flow-chart" and answering the questions below, track some of the consequences in your life.

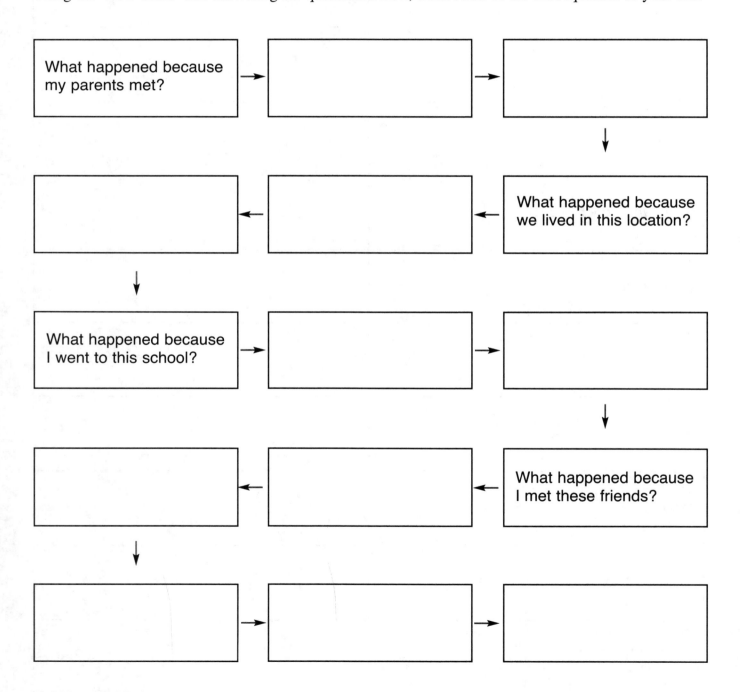

Any Questions?

When you finished reading *The Tale of Despereaux*, did you have questions that were left unanswered? Write a few of your questions on the back of this page.

Work in groups or by yourself to predict possible answers for all or some of the questions you have asked above, as well as those written below. When you have finished, share your predictions with your class.

1. Does Despereaux return to live with his parents and siblings?_____

2. Does the Mouse Council send Despereaux to the dungeon again? _____

3. Do Roscuro and Despereaux become friends? _____

4. Do Miggery Sow and Princess Pea become friends? _____

5. Does King Phillip remarry? _____

6. What happens to Miggery Sow as an adult? _____

7. Does Princess Pea get married? If so, how does Despereaux feel about this? _____

8. Does Antoinette have any more mouse babies? _____

9. Does the Cook get in trouble for making soup? _____

10. Does King Phillip decide that soup is legal again? _____

11. Does Despereaux fall in love with another mouse? _____

12. What happens to Botticelli Remorso?

_____

13. What does King Phillip say when he sees his daughter eating soup with a mouse and a rat?

_____

14. Does Despereaux become a writer of fairy tales?_____

15. What else does Princess Pea depict in the tapestry of her life? _____

16. Does the Cook ever see Despereaux again in her kitchen? _____ If so, what does she do?

_____

17. What happens to Despereaux's brother, Furlough? _____

18. Does Hovis, the threadmaster, get to meet the Princess? _____

19. Does King Phillip allow Despereaux and Roscuro to live upstairs in the palace? _____

Book Report Ideas

There are several ways to report on a book after you have read it. When you have finished *The Tale of Despereaux*, choose a method of reporting from the list below or come up with your own idea on how best to report on this book.

Design a Book Jacket

Design a book jacket for this book. On the front, draw a picture that you feel best captures this story. On the back, write a paragraph or two which summarizes the main points of this book. Don't forget to write the title and the author's name.

Make a Time Line

On paper, create time lines to show the significant events in the main characters' lives. You may illustrate your time lines, as well.

Create a Scrapbook

Use magazine pictures, photographs, and other illustrations to create a scrapbook that the characters might use to document their lives. They might choose to decorate their scrapbooks with soup recipes or pictures of knights and princesses. Perhaps they would fill their scrapbooks with bits of red thread, or pieces of tapestry, or sketches of mice!

Make a Collage

Using old magazines and photographs, design a collage that illustrates the characters' adventures in *The Tale of Despereaux*.

Create a Time Capsule

What items might the characters put in a time capsule for someone else to find later? What container might they use as a time capsule?

Write a Biography

Do research to find out about the life of author, Kate DiCamillo. You may use the Internet or magazines. Write a biography, showing how Ms. DiCamillo's life experiences might have influenced this novel.

Act Out a Play

With one or two other students, write a play featuring some of the characters in this novel. Then act out your play for your class.

Make Puppets

Using a variety of materials, design puppets to represent one or all of the characters in this novel. You may decide to work with other students to write and perform a puppet show for your class. Consider performing your show for an Open House at your school!

Research Ideas

As you read *The Tale of Despereaux*, you discovered ideas, events, people, and animals about which you might wish to know more. To increase your understanding of the characters, places, and events in this novel, do research to discover additional information.

Work alone or in groups to learn about one or more of the items listed below. You may use books, magazines, encyclopedias, documentary films, and/or the Internet. Afterwards, share your findings with your class.

- knights
- castles
- dungeons
- famous royal families
- mice
- rats
- the feudal system
- famous royal cooks
- tapestry-making
- the history of soup
- clothing worn by princesses
- fairy tales
- famous non-conformists
- courtly love
- chiaroscuro in art
- hypnotism
- child abandonment
- juggling
- guitars
- child abuse
- stained-glass windows
- candle making
- Kate DiCamillo
- motherless children
- Newbery Award
- the historical significance of handkerchiefs
- servants
- prejudice
- famous non-conformists

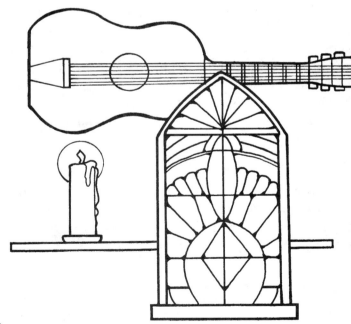

Field Trips and Class Visits

Now that your students have learned about rats and mice and castles and fairy tales, they may enjoy taking one or more field trips related to these subjects. In addition, you may want to invite guests to visit your class.

Choose an activity from the list below, and locate the appropriate contact person in the phone book to arrange a visit. Be sure to call at least two weeks in advance to give the staff, or your classroom guest, plenty of time to prepare for a visit.

Rats Versus Mice

Some students may never have seen a real mouse or rat close up. Visit a local pet store, zoo, or animal shelter to learn more about these rodents. Or ask an expert to visit your class with caged rats and mice in order to explain the habits of and differences between the two types of mammals.

Fairy Tales

Invite a local children's author to visit your classroom and talk about his/her books, explaining the process of writing them and getting them published. Ask if the author will lead your students in writing their own fairy tale. Alternatively, visit a library with a good selection of fairy tales and arrange for the children's librarian to read his/her favorites aloud. One tale relevant to *The Tale of Despereaux* is *Stone Soup*.

Fun in the Kitchen

Ask a local restaurant to allow you to tour the kitchen during off-hours. Students will marvel at the enormous pots and pans, the hours spent preparing food for dozens of people, and the large quantities of ingredients. Or invite a local chef to visit your classroom, to discuss the joys and challenges of cooking for large

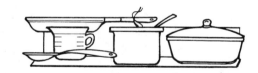

groups of people. Students may choose to ask questions of the visiting chef, pertaining to the Cook in *The Tale of Despereaux*. The chef may lead students in the creation of a fabulous soup, as well!

Tapestry-Making

Students have a chance, in this book, to create tapestry bookmarkers. You might choose to invite a local weaver and/or seamstress to visit your classroom in order to teach students skills. Alternatively, visit a local art or natural history museum to view tapestries and other weaving and/or needlework from long ago.

Knights and Maidens

The Society of Creative Anachronism is a group dedicated to researching and recreating the world before the 17th century. Go to their website, **http://www.sca.org**, to locate a local chapter. Invite members to speak to your students about knights and maidens and courtly love, or arrange for your students to visit one of the Society's events.

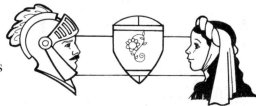

Costume Party!

Why not host a costume party in your classroom, to celebrate The Tale of Despereaux? Your students will enjoy planning, preparing for, and participating in their party.

Party Checklist

Three weeks before the party. . .

❏ Decide when and where your party will occur.

❏ Think of a theme for the party. Themes related to *The Tale of Despereaux* include Fairy Tales, Mice and Rats, and Knights and Castles. Discuss costumes and activities related to your chosen theme. Will you have a costume contest? Stage a play, mock trial, or puppet show.

❏ Talk about whom you want to invite. Will you invite another class in your grade or treat a younger class to a story-telling party? Will you offer the party as part of your school's Open House and invite parents and siblings? Make and send the invitations on page 40.

❏ Discuss decorations. Will you display students' hand-made handkerchiefs, tapestries, copper books, and dioramas? What other decorations will complement your chosen theme?

Two weeks before the party. . .

❏ Decide what food and drink you will make as a class. This book provides recipes for chicken-watercress-garlic soup, "Ants on a Log," tortilla triangles, and carrot bars (page 41). You may also want to offer bread or crackers.

❏ Pass around a sign-up sheet. Each student should be encouraged to bring something unique to the party. They might bring food, sign up to play the guitar or juggle, read stories, or teach guests to sew tapestries.

❏ Send home a note to students' parents to remind them of the party, and to let them know what the student has signed up to bring.

One week before the party. . .

❏ Send home a note reminding students of what they are to bring for the party.

❏ Buy and/or make decorations.

The day before the party. . .

❏ Make chicken-watercress-garlic soup and other refreshments.

The day of the party. . .

❏ Decorate the party space and set up storytelling, juggling, and/or sewing areas.

Enjoy!

Costume Party! (cont.)

You're Invited to
a Costume Party!

Day: _____

Time: _____

Place: _____

Hosts: _____

Theme: _____

Foods Fit for a Rodent

Mice and rats love many foods; among their favorites are cheese, carrots and celery, and bread. Below, you'll find fun foods to make in honor of Despereaux and Roscuro!

Ants on a Log

Ingredients

celery stalks   raisins or chocolate chips
cream cheese (or non-dairy cream cheese)   knife

Directions

Cut celery into 3" pieces. Spread the inside of each piece with cream cheese. Place four raisins or chocolate chips on top, and enjoy!

Tortilla Triangles

Ingredients

corn or flour tortillas   cheese   black olives   oven or toaster oven

Directions

Grate cheese and sprinkle over one tortilla. Sprinkle chopped black olives over the cheese. Place tortilla under broiler until cheese bubbles. When tortilla is cool, cut into triangles and serve.

Carrot Bars

Ingredients For Cake:

1 ½ cups flour	¼ tsp. nutmeg	2 cups grated carrots
1 ½ tsp. cinnamon	2 eggs	8 oz. crushed pineapple in juice, drained
½ tsp. baking powder	½ cup packed brown sugar	
½ tsp. salt	⅓ cup vegetable oil	

For Topping:

1 cup whipped cream cheese	grated carrots (optional)	wire rack
2 Tbs. powdered sugar	two bowls	knife
	whisk	13" x 9" baking pan

Directions

1. Heat oven to 350°F. Grease a 13" x 9" baking pan. In bowl, combine flour, cinnamon, baking powder, salt, and nutmeg; set aside. In large bowl, whisk together eggs, brown sugar, and oil until well blended. Stir in carrots, pineapple, and flour mixture until combined. Spread batter evenly in pan.
2. Bake until top is set and edges pull away from pan, about 25 minutes. Transfer pan to rack and cool. Cut into 12 bars.
3. For topping: In small bowl, blend together cream cheese and sugar until creamy. Put a spoonful of topping onto each bar, and top with grated carrots, if desired.

Note to Teacher: Send home a written note with students, inquiring about pertinent food allergies, well in advance of preparing food. Make sure that students have adult supervision when cutting, grating and cooking.

Adopt a Class Rat or Mouse

Rats and mice make wonderful pets. You can adopt one from your local animal shelter and care for it in your classroom. Here are some details to keep in mind before you adopt a class pet.

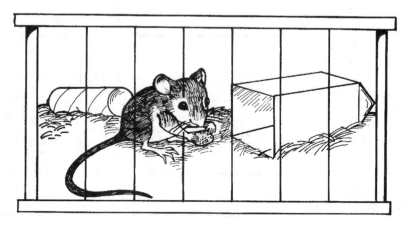

Shelter

Your rat or mouse will need a roomy cage in which to live. Make sure to cover the bottom of the cage with wood shavings or newspaper, and change this daily. Rodents like hiding places—a simple cardboard tube or milk carton provides a fine "cave." If possible, also provide an exercise wheel on which your rat or mouse can play.

Food

Pet stores sell specially-formulated pellets designed to give rats and mice the nutrients they need to stay healthy. Feed your pet according to the directions on the package, and offer supplemental snacks— carrots, celery, crackers—sparingly.

Water

Animals, like humans, need constant access to fresh water. Make sure to keep a shallow dish of water in your pet's cage, and change it daily.

Other Details

Rats and mice are remarkable breeders. If you choose to adopt two rodents, make sure both are male, or both are female, so that you don't find yourself searching for homes for an abundance of babies!

Consider taking your class pet home on weekends. Teachers can allow students to take turns caring for the rat on weekends and during vacations from school.

Always move and speak quietly around a rat or mouse. With proper care and loving attention, rodents can grow quite tame, allowing people to pick them up and pet them and even feed them by hand.

Objective Test and Essay

Matching: Match the description of each character with his or her name.

1. Despereaux
2. Roscuro
3. Princess Pea
4. Miggery Sow
5. Gregory
6. Queen Rosemary
7. King Philip
8. Botticelli Remorso
9. Antoinette
10. the Cook

a. says the meaning of life is suffering

b. says "adieu" when her son is sent to the dungeon

c. dies while eating a bowl of delicious soup

d. falls in love with Princess Pea

e. makes soup even though it's illegal

f. swings from a chandelier and falls into soup

g. offers a bowl of soup to a rat

h. sold into slavery by her father

i. outlaws soup and mourns for his wife

j. dies in the dungeon after his rope is cut

True or False: Answer true or false on the blank lines below.

_____ 1. Miggery Sow and Princess Pea both want their mothers.

_____ 2. King Phillip is a mean person.

_____ 3. Botticelli Remorso tells Despereaux not to kill Roscuro.

_____ 4. Despereaux's father accompanies him to the dungeon.

_____ 5. Lester, Antoinette, and Furlough discover Despereaux eating soup with the princess.

Short Answer: On a separate sheet of paper, write a brief response to each question, using complete sentences.

1. Why does Lester allow his son to be taken to the dungeon?

2. Why does Roscuro decide to inflict suffering upon others?

3. How does Princess Pea treat Miggery Sow?

4. Why does the Cook give Despereaux a bowl of soup?

5. Why doesn't Princess Pea want Roscuro to be killed?

Essay: Respond to the following on a separate sheet of paper.
Despereaux forgives his father for sending him to the dungeon. What other characters are forgiven for their hurtful actions in this book? Who forgives them?

Response

On a separate sheet of paper, explain and respond to the following quotations as selected by your teacher.

Chapter One: "I will name this mouse Despereaux, for all the sadness, for the many despairs in this place.'"

Chapter Two: "'He was listening, with his big ears, to the sweet sound that no other mouse seemed to hear."

Chapter Six: "'Don't you understand?' shouted Lester. 'He must be punished. He must be brought up before the tribunal.'"

Chapter Eleven: "'He would do as the threadmaster had suggested. He would be brave for the princess."

Chapter Fifteen: "'Spoons. Bowls. Kettles. All of them gathered here as hard evidence of the pain of loving a living thing.'"

Chapter Eighteen: "He wanted to be filled, flooded, blinded again with light."

Chapter Twenty-one: "If the rat had not looked over his shoulder, perhaps his heart would not have broken."

Chapter Twenty-four: "'Go on, Mig,' he said. 'You belong to that man now.'"

Chapter Twenty-six: "Looking at the royal family had awakened some deep and slumbering need in her; it was as if a small candle had been lit in her interior, sparked to life by the brilliance of the king and the queen and the princess."

Chapter Twenty-eight: "'You will be a servant!' shouted the soldier. 'Not a slave!'"

Chapter Thirty-two: "The knight stopped swinging his sword. He looked at Despereaux. 'You know me,' he said."

Chapter Thirty-three: "Instead, he reached into his pocket and then held his napkin up to this face and sneezed into it, once, twice, three times."

Chapter Thirty-five: "'I have not forgotten, Mama,' she whispered. 'I have not forgotten you. I have not forgotten soup.'"

Chapter Forty: "Isn't it ridiculous to think that a mouse could ever forgive anyone for such perfidy?"

Chapter Forty-five: "'Mouse,' said Cook, 'would you like some soup?'"

Chapter Forty-seven: "And so the mouse reached out. He took hold of the rat's tail."

Chapter Fifty-two: "But the rat, in seeking forgiveness, did manage to shed some small light, some happiness into another life."

Conversations

Work in groups according to the numbers in parentheses to write or act out the conversations that might have occurred in *The Tale of Despereaux*.

- Antoinette and Lester argue over whether Despereaux should have been punished for speaking to humans. (2 people)

- Despereaux tells Gregory a story in order to save himself. (2 people)

- King Phillip explains to his daughter why mice shouldn't live in the house. (2 people)

- The threadmaster and Despereaux have a conversation about fairy tales and courtly love. (2 people)

- The new prisoner tells Botticelli Remorso and Roscuro what happened to his family. (3 people)

- King Phillip explains to his daughter why he has outlawed soup. (2 people)

- Miggery Sow's father and Uncle bargain for her. (2 people)

- The prisoner meets his daughter, Miggery Sow, in the dungeon. (2 people)

- Queen Rosemary speaks to Princess Pea in a dream. (2 people)

- Despereaux and Roscuro discuss their feelings for Princess Pea. (2 people)

- The Cook and Louise speak to King Phillip about Miggery Sow. (3 people)

- Princess Pea and Miggery Sow reminisce about their mothers. (2 people)

- Lester and Desperaux meet and talk about forgiveness. (2 people)

- Despereaux tells Princess Pea about meeting Gregory in the dungeon. (2 people)

- The rats in the dungeon discuss Roscuro's kidnapping of the princess and why Roscuro wasn't killed. (3 people or more)

- Roscuro explains to Princess Pea why he wanted to make her suffer. (2 people)

- Princess Pea, King Phillip, Miggery Sow, Roscuro, and Despereaux enjoy a bowl of soup together. (5 people)

Fiction

Andersen, Hans Christian. *Complete Hans Christian Andersen Fairy Tales.* (Derrydale, 1993)

Brothers Grimm. *Complete Brothers Grimm Fairy Tales.* (Grammercy, 1993)

Cleary, Beverly. *The Mouse and the Motorcycle.* (HarperTrophy, 1990)

Creech, Sharon. *Granny Torrelli Makes Soup.* (Joanna Cotler, 2003)

D e Saint-Exupery, Antoine. *The Little Prince.* (Harvest, 2000)

DiCamillo, Kate. *Because of Winn-Dixie.* (Candlewick, 2001)

DiCamillo, Kate. *The Tiger Rising.* (Candlewick, 2002)

Funke, Cornelia. *Inkheart.* (Chicken House, 2003)

Green, Roger Lancelyn. *King Arthur and his Knights of the Round Table.* (Puffin, 1995)

Levine, Gail Carson. *Ella Enchanted.* (HarperTrophy, 1998)

Lewis, C.S. *The Lion, the Witch, and the Wardrobe.* (HarperTrophy, 2000)

O'Brien, Robert C. *Mrs. Frisby and the Rats of Nimh.* (Aladdin, 1986)

Snicket, Lemony. *The Slippery Slope.* (HarperCollins, 2003)

Spinelli, Jerry. *Milkweed.* (Knopf, 2003)

Nonfiction

Conniff, Richard. Rats: *The Good, the Bad, and the Ugly.* (Crown Books for Young Readers, 2002)

Fowler, Allan. *Mice and Rats.* (Children's Press, 1999)

Langley, Andrew. *Eyewitness: Medieval Life.* (D.K. Publishing, 2000)

MacDonald, Fiona. *How Would You Survive in the Middle Ages?* (Franklin Watts, 1997)

Osborne, Will and Ma. *Knights and Castles.* (Random House Books for Young Readers, 2000)

Vidner, Bradley. *All About Your Mouse.* (Barron's Educational Series, 1999)

Answer Key

Page 10
1. Antoinette is disappointed because only one of her babies lived, and she is afraid Despereaux will die, as well.
2. Despereaux has large ears, he is born with his eyes open, and he is not interested in searching for crumbs or nibbling paper.
3. Furlough tries to teach Despereaux how to scurry, and Merlot tries to teach him how to nibble on books.
4. Despereaux can't nibble on the book because he wants to read the story told in its pages.
5. Despereaux reveals himself to the King and the Princess because he is entranced by the King's music.
6. When Pea smiles at Despereaux, he falls in love.
7. The other mice say Despereaux cannot be trusted because he has allowed humans to see and touch him, and humans cannot be trusted.
8. Lester believes his son cannot be trusted, and he is afraid Despereaux will be the end of the mouse community.

Page 15
1. Despereaux's mother faints, and then bids her son "adieu."
2. Despereaux discovers that one of the hoods is his brother.
3. Gregory is the jailer.
4. Gregory asked Despereaux to tell him a story.
5. Roscuro goes upstairs to the party because he loves the light.
6. Queen Rosemary dies from the shock of seeing a rat in her soup.
7. Roscuro doesn't like being called a rat because it sounds like a curse and an insult.
8. Roscuro's heart breaks when he looks over his shoulder at Princess Pea.

Page 18
The Tower of London was located in London, built in the 11th century by William the Conqueror. Several monarchs, including the 13-year old King Edward V, were held and killed here.

The Kaiserburg Castle is located in Nurumberg, Germany, built in three stages between the 11th and 15th centuries—initially, by Emperor Heinrich III. A succession of German emperors lived in the Castle. The robber knight Eppelein von Gailingen was held prisoner here.

The Bastille was built in Paris, France, in 1370 as a defense against the English. Charles VI turned it into a prison to hold political prisoners considered a threat to the royal court.

Mamertine Prison was built in the seventh century, and was located in Rome under the city's sewers. Legend holds that Saint Peter and Saint Paul were held here.

Extra Credit.: The top level was built by Ancus, the bottom level by Servius Tullins.

Page 20
1. Miggery Sow's ears swell and grow cauliflower-shaped from being hit. She also goes partially deaf.
2. Miggery's father is the prisoner who lives in the dungeon.
3. Miggery feels hope and excitement after she sees the royal family.
4. Miggery is sent to the castle because the soldier takes her away from Uncle, but her father is gone.
5. Miggery and Princess Pea are the same age, and they have both lost their mother.
6. Miggery is a poor servant who is not very bright, and Princess Pea is a rich princess who is articulate and compassionate.
7. Miggery can't smell the dungeon's stench or hear the frightening noises inside it.
8. Students may guess that Despereaux is hiding in Gregory's napkin; give points for all reasonable answers.

Page 25
1. Miggery Sow takes Despereaux's tail.
2. Miggery believes in Roscuro's plan because she's not very bright, and she wants to be a princess very badly.
3. Princess Pea dreams that her mother feeds her soup.
4. The princess feels sorry for Miggery because the servant girl wants to be a princes badly.
5. Roscuro chews through Gregory's rope, and the jailer loses his way in the dungeon and dies.
6. Despereaux forgives his father to stop his own heart from breaking.
7. The king believes rodents are liars and thieves.
8. Despereaux wants the spool of red thread so that he doesn't get lost in the dungeon.

Page 27
1. Odysseus attempted to return to his home in Ithaca. He faced numerous challenges—monsters and temptations and interferences from the gods before finally returning home.
2. Joan of Arc believed God told her to help lead the French to victory over the English. She did do this, but went on to conduct further operations against the English without the permission of French officials. She was tried for heresy and burned at the stake.

Answer Key

3. Sir Galahad was one of the Knights of the Round Table, sent by King Arthur to search for the Holy Grail. To prove himself worthy, he had to pull a sword from a stone. Upon finding the Grail, he was overcome with ecstasy and died.

4. Amelia Earhart wanted to fly around the world in her airplane. Her plane broke down on one occasion, and she most likely did not accomplish her goal, as she and her partner disappeared and were never found again.

5. Mahatma Gandhi wanted to bring about Indian independence from British rule. He did help to accomplish this goal, in spite of being imprisoned by British authorities periodically and being threatened by assassination attempts. He was murdered by an assassin in 1948.

6. Harriet Tubman worked for African American freedom, helping to bring many slaves to freedom through the Underground Railroad. She did accomplish her goals, in spite of a constant threat of capture.

Page 30

1. The Cook is glad to see Despereaux in her kitchen because she is relieved that he is not the king or another official person who will catch her making soup.

2. The Cook's laughter hurts Despereaux perhaps because he is reminded of how small and harmless he is. Give points for all reasonable answers.

3. The Cook gives Despereaux a bowl of soup so he can taste it and warm his heart.

4. Despereaux follows Botticelli Remorso because the rat promised to take him to the princess.

5. Despereaux notices human and mouse bones, fur, red thread, and a group of rats following him.

6. The Princess asked Miggery Sow what she wants.

7. Miggery Sow wants her mother.

8. Princess Pea offers Roscuro a bowl of soup to stop her own heart from breaking.

Page 33

Mon Dieu = My God
merlot = type of red wine
furlough = leave of absence
C'est moi? = Is it me?
oui = yes
chiaroscuro = arrangement of light and dark in painting
Antoinette = Marie Antoinette, Queen of France
Princess Pea = The Princess and the Pea by Hans

Christian Andersen
Despereaux = the root may be "despair," to lose hope

Page 43
Matching

1. d	6. c
2. f	7. i
3. g	8. a
4. h	9. b
5. j	10. e

True or False

1. True
2. False
3. True
4. False
5. True

Short Answer

1. Lester allows his son to be taken to the dungeon because he believes Despereaux can't be trusted and will cause the demise of the mouse community.

2. Roscuro decides to inflict suffering upon others because Princess Pea called him a rat, and his heart broke from the insult.

3. Princess Pea treats Miggery Sow with kindness and compassion.

4. The Cook gives Despereaux a bowl of soup because she believes soup needs another mouth to taste it and that soup will warm the mouse's heart.

5. Princess Pea doesn't want Roscuro to be killed because she forgives him for kidnapping her, and she doesn't want her heart to be broken.

Essay

Answers will vary. Accept reasonable and well-supported answers.

Page 44

Grade students on their comprehension of the story as evidence by the lengths of answers and depths of responses.

Page 45

Grade students on comprehension of the story, knowledge of the characters, and creativity.